SEATTLE
SEAHAWKS

Richard Rambeck

CREATIVE ⚫ EDUCATION INC.

Published by Creative Education, Inc.
123 S. Broad Street, Mankato, Minnesota 56001

Designed by Rita Marshall
Cover illustration by Lance Hidy Associates
Photos by Allsport, Duomo, Focus On Sports, FPG,
Spectra-Action, Sportschrome and Wide World Photos

Library of Congress Cataloging-in-Publication Data

Rambeck, Richard.
  The Seattle Seahawks/Richard Rambeck.
  p.   cm.
  ISBN 0-88682-384-6
  1. Seattle Seahawks (Football team)—History.   I. Title.
GV956.S4R36   1990
796.332'64'09797772—dc20   90-41209
                                                    CIP

Seattle has been called the most livable city in the United States. One reason why Seattle stands out is that it is a busy city surrounded by natural wonders. It has waterways on almost every side, including Puget Sound to the west and Lake Washington to the east. Mountains rise above the city as well, most notably the legendary Mount Rainier, which dominates the southeastern sky.

Within this beautiful environment is the population and trade center of the Pacific Northwest. Goods from Japan and the rest of Asia flow through the Port of Seattle. Goods from the United States are often loaded onto ships heading for the Far East. This trading activity was one of the main

An early Seahawk star, running back Al Hunter.

The Seahawk logo depicts the noble hawk which proud Northwest Indians used on ancient totem poles.

reasons Seattle grew quickly in the 1940s and 1950s. The cities around Seattle also grew rapidly in the 1960s and 1970s. The Puget Sound area was booming.

In the early 1970s, business leaders from Seattle began pushing hard for a National Football League franchise. In November 1972 construction started on the Kingdome, a sixty-five-thousand-seat indoor stadium that was designed to be ideal for both football and baseball. In 1974 NFL officials announced that Seattle would be allowed to join the league beginning in the 1976 season. Seattle, which had long supported college football, would now have a chance to support a professional team.

An ownership group for the Seattle team was formed, and one of its first jobs was to choose a nickname. A public contest was held, and more than twenty thousand people sent in suggestions. The winning nickname, chosen by 151 people, was "Seahawks." (A seahawk is a type of bird similar to a gull.) No other U.S. professional team in any sport had ever had that nickname. "Seahawks" was an unusual name, but this was going to be an unusual team. It would be a team that would be successful in an unusually short time. It would be a team that would win in unusual ways, using unusual plays. And it would be a team that would create an unusually strong bond with its fans, a bond that would make the Seahawks one of the best-supported teams in the NFL.

Before the Seahawks ever played a game, they became one of the hottest tickets in the city. The team sold more than 58,000 season tickets, and then the team management refused to sell any more. There had to be at least some tickets available for fans who couldn't afford to buy season passes.

The "Seahawks" celebrate a victory.

THE EXPANSION YEARS: ZORN TO BE WILD

Jack Patera was named as the Seahawks' first head coach.

The Seattle fans got their first chance to see the Seahawks in a preseason contest against the San Francisco 49ers in the Kingdome on August 1, 1976. A full house watched Seattle fall behind early, and then rally behind a left-handed, first-year quarterback named Jim Zorn. Zorn brought the Seahawks to within a touchdown, 27-20, and was driving the team as the clock wound down. With the crowd roaring, Zorn nearly pulled it off. He was tackled on the 49er two yard line on the game's final play.

The Seahawks had lost, but the fans didn't care. They stood and gave the team—their team—a standing ovation. Many of the cheers were for Zorn, a player who had been unwanted by the other NFL teams. But Zorn was a typical Seattle star: he was unusual. Most teams have quarterbacks who were picked high in the college draft. Zorn wasn't drafted, by the Seahawks or by anybody else. He was a little-known quarterback from a small college, California Poly at Pomona, hardly USC, UCLA, or Notre Dame.

Zorn came to Seattle as a free agent, after spending a year on injured reserve with the Dallas Cowboys. The Los Angeles Rams were interested in Zorn, but he signed with Seattle, believing that he'd have a better chance with a new team. When the Seahawks' first training camp started, there were nine quarterbacks trying out. A few of them had experience playing with other NFL teams. Zorn only had experience watching the Dallas Cowboys practice. But Zorn had something special; he was different. When he showed up for the first time at the Seahawks' training camp, he was driving an old yellow Volkswagen. Quarterbacks usually own expensive sports cars.

The Seattle coaches immediately noticed something unusual about Zorn: he didn't just drop back and throw the ball. He'd drop back, and when things broke down, he'd take off running, usually to his left. He'd either throw it or run—and he could really run. Zorn told newspaper reporters that during summer vacations in high school, he ran around and threw balls at a baseball backstop. That, he said, was how he developed his unique style.

Pro scouts said Zorn was too wild, too unpredictable. But that was the secret of his success. During preseason in the Seahawks' first year, other quarterbacks tried to make the offense go by using the usual methods. Zorn did the unusual—and succeeded. Seattle's first star had been born. And Coach Jack Patera had his quarterback.

Four weeks after the loss to San Francisco, Zorn directed Seattle to its first victory: a 17-16 triumph over the San Diego Chargers in a preseason game. Typically, Zorn did it the unusual way, throwing a touchdown pass to tight end Ron Howard with thirteen seconds left. (Like Zorn, Howard was an unusual player; in college at Seattle University, he had played basketball, not football.) When the regular season started, Zorn continued his heroics by nearly leading the first-year Seahawks to victories over St. Louis and Green Bay. In the season's sixth week, Seattle got its first regular season victory, beating another expansion team, Tampa Bay, 13-10.

The Seahawks' first year ended with a 2-12 record, not bad by expansion-team standards. Zorn threw for more than 2,500 yards, Sherman Smith led the team in rushing with 537 yards, and a young receiver named Steve Largent was Seattle's top pass catcher, with fifty-four receptions for 705 yards.

1 9 7 6

On November 7, Sherman Smith became the first Seattle back to rush for over 100 yards in a game.

A Seattle legend—running back Curt Warner, (pages 10–11).

The following season, 1977, began poorly. The Seahawks lost their first four games, and then lost Zorn because of an injury. But Zorn came back and led the Seahawks to five victories, a record for a second-year expansion team.

1 9 7 7

After missing four games with injuries, Jim Zorn led the 'Hawks to a 56-14 victory over Buffalo.

LARGENT AND THE SEAHAWKS CATCH ON

In 1978, the exciting Seahawks almost set the pro football world on its ear. The team, led by the passing of Jim Zorn, the rushing of Sherman Smith, and the receiving of Steve Largent, nearly won the Western Division of the American Football Conference. The Seahawks also almost made the playoffs. They finished with a 9-7 record, only one game behind Denver in the AFC West. Zorn set team records for passes attempted, passes completed, and yards gained. Smith gained 805 yards rushing. But it was Largent who had the best year. He caught seventy-one passes for 1,168 yards and eight touchdowns, and he was named to the Pro Bowl.

On a team of unusual players with unusual backgrounds, Largent fit right in. Unlike Zorn, Largent actually was drafted, but not by the Seahawks. The Houston Oilers took Largent, who had led the nation's college receivers in touchdown catches both in 1974 and 1975 while at Tulsa, in the fourth round of the 1976 NFL draft. The Oilers apparently weren't very impressed with Largent's abilities, because they traded him to Seattle during the 1976 preseason for an eighth-round pick in the 1977 draft.

Thirteen years after that trade, Largent retired owning every important pass-receiving record in NFL history. He is certain to be elected to the Pro Football Hall of Fame when he becomes eligible in 1994. But it's not impossible to understand why Houston gave up on Largent. He wasn't fast; in fact, his forty yard dash time was considered slow compared with times turned in by the speed burners who are on every NFL roster at wide receiver.

Largent wasn't fast, but he was quick. Lester Hayes, a former all-pro cornerback with the Los Angeles Raiders, said that Largent had the quickest ankles in the world. Largent might not have been able to outrun defenders, but he was able to use his quickness to get away from them. Even Hayes, who called Largent the best receiver ever, had a hard time at first believing Largent was any good. "He didn't look like a receiver, he looked like an insurance salesman," Hayes said. "I thought I should be able to dominate this guy. But, I'll tell you what, he is God's gift. I've covered everybody in the NFL, all those high-speed guys. But I never covered anybody who gave me as many problems as Steve Largent did."

Why was Largent so good? He worked at it, constantly. "I've never seen anyone spend more time at preparation," said Fred Biletnikoff, a former Oakland Raider receiver who is considered one of the best pass catchers ever. "Steve Largent is a role model not just for kids, but for NFL players everywhere. Few if any have the dedication he has."

Steve Largent led the Seahawks in pass catches and in yardage every year from 1976 through 1987, an achievement unmatched by any other receiver with any other team. Eight times, he had more than 1,000 yards receiving in a season, an NFL record. He had at least fifty catches in ten seasons; nobody else had that many catches more than seven times. He caught passes in 177 straight regular sea-

1 9 7 8

Defensive back Keith Simpson from Memphis State was the Seahawks' first pick in the college draft.

13

Seahawk in Pro Bowl? Steve Largent, the first Seahawk to make a Pro Bowl, caught a record setting five passes.

son games. And he caught more passes, for more yardage, and for more touchdowns than anyone who ever played the game.

But Steve Largent, like his buddy Zorn, was more than a football player to the Seattle Seahawks. He was a team leader, he had the respect of every teammate and every opponent, and he spent much of his time off from football doing charity work. The NFL named Largent its Man of the Year in 1988 for his many activities in the community. "Steve Largent is just one of those amazing people," said Mary Ann Ranta of Children's Hospital in Seattle, where Largent has done a lot of charity work. "Whenever something comes up where we'd really appreciate his involvement, he's always been there for us. He is such a hero to so many people."

When Steve Largent was introduced in enemy stadiums, the crowd didn't boo him, even though they knew Largent was probably going to be a thorn in the side of the home team. They cheered his achievements, although not as loudly as the fans in Seattle cheered. When Largent caught his one-hundredth career touchdown pass against the Cincinnati Bengals in 1989, the Cincinnati crowd started to boo. Then, suddenly, the Bengal fans realized who had caught the pass and what it meant. Largent had made history again, and they had been a part of it. The boos became cheers. Steve Largent had no enemies, only admirers.

Largent and Zorn had great years in 1978, and even better years in 1979. Largent had 1,237 yards receiving, and Zorn threw for 3,661 yards, both club records. The Seahawks finished 9-7 again, and although they didn't make the playoffs, they made their first appearance on Monday Night Football something to remember. Every

Like Steve Largent, John L. Williams (#32) is a team leader.

With 93 points, kicker Efron Herrera was the scoring leader for a lean season.

team wants to play on Monday Night Football, because it's an opportunity to play on national television while all the other players in the league watch. It's a chance to show off, and the Seahawks took their chance and ran with it . . . but not at first.

Playing the Atlanta Falcons in Atlanta, the Seahawks fell behind 14-0, but then Zorn, Largent, and a running back named Dan Doornick came alive. Zorn threw passes to everyone, including one to kicker Efren Herrera on a fake field goal. Largent showed the TV audience why he was Pro Bowl material. And Doornink rushed for 122 yards and two touchdowns. (Doornink was another one of the Seahawks' unusual stars. He wasn't just a football player; he was a medical student and would become a doctor when his NFL career ended.)

Seattle used every trick in the book, including an onside kick in the third quarter. It worked, and the Seahawks converted it into a touchdown. When Herrera caught his pass from Zorn, ABC broadcaster Howard Cosell exclaimed, "These Seahawks are just having fun playing football." Not only did they have fun, they also defeated the Falcons 31-28.

But the Seahawks fell on hard times in 1980. The team's streak of success came abruptly to a halt. Seattle lost all eight of its home games, despite the fact that all were sold out. The team finished 4-12 and in last place in the AFC West. The following year the Seahawks improved a little, finishing 6-10, but they still wound up last in the five-team AFC West. In 1982 the NFL season was interrupted by a players' strike, and seven of the games were canceled. Seattle finished 4-5. It was Coach Jack Patera's last season.

CHUCK AND THE MAN FROM MILTON

In 1983 a new coach, Chuck Knox, took over the team. Knox had built championship-quality teams for the Los Angeles Rams and Buffalo Bills. He had a reputation as a guy who could turn losers into winners. When Knox came to Seattle, he told people it would take time to build a winner. Seattle, after all, hadn't had a winning season in four years. The team was 14-27 since 1979.

Knox believed in old-time football. He believed that a good running game combined with a mistake-free offense and a solid defense that could cause fumbles and interceptions added up to victory. The Seahawks desperately needed a really good running back to make Knox's offense go. They hadn't had a quality back since Sherman Smith in the late 1970s. Knox set out to change that.

On the day of the 1983 draft, Seattle made a daring trade with the Houston Oilers, the same team that had traded Steve Largent to the Seahawks. Seattle sent its first-, second- and third-round draft choices to Houston for the Oilers' first-round pick, which was the third pick in the draft. The Seahawks would have a shot at drafting a great young back. Knox selected Penn State running back Curt Warner, who led his college team to a national championship in 1982. The Seahawks had their star running back.

Knox also built a defense that caused a record number of mistakes by the opposition in the next five years. The pieces of Knox's championship puzzle were coming together, but there was one more that had to fall into place: a quarterback. Jim Zorn was still around, but his gambling style didn't suit Knox. Zorn's high-powered offense often

1 9 8 3

Aerial wizardry by Dave Krieg yielded a record setting 418 yards on November 20, against Denver.

The high powered Seattle offense digs in, (pages 18–19).

Rookie running back Curt Warner led the AFC and was second overall in NFL rushing yardage.

won games for Seattle when the defense couldn't, but Zorn tended to throw a lot of interceptions. Knox believed he had a defense that could win games if the offense didn't make too many mistakes.

By the middle of the 1983 season, Knox was ready to make a change. And in typical Seahawk style, the change featured an unusual player. If you met Dave Kreig on the street, you'd never believe he was a National Football League quarterback. You'd never believe that he was one of the highest-rated quarterbacks in NFL history. And you'd never believe where Dave Kreig came from. Kreig came from a college that actually closed down a few years after he left, Milton College in Wisconsin. Dave Kreig is the only quarterback—and the only player, for that matter—from Milton who ever played in the NFL.

So in the middle of the 1983 season, Knox decided that the Man from Milton was the guy to lead the Seahawks. "Dave Kreig is one of those natural-born leader types," said Reggie McKenzie, a former Seahawk offensive lineman. "He comes into a game all jacked up. His enthusiasm spills over and splashes on everyone else." Kreig led Seattle to five victories in the last eight games of the regular season. That strong finish gave the Seahawks a 9-7 record and a spot in the playoffs.

Seattle didn't win the AFC West, but the Seahawks made it to the playoffs as a wildcard team. On Christmas Eve, the Seahawks gave their fans a big present, a 31-7 victory over Denver in Seattle's first playoff game. On New Year's Eve, the Seahawks played their second playoff game ever. It was a game they were given no chance to win. The Miami

Dolphins, who were playing at home, were supposed to beat Seattle badly. One Miami newspaper columnist even called the underdog Seahawks the "Sea-Whos."

Miami led the "Sea-Whos" 20-17 late in the fourth quarter. But then Kreig completed two big passes to Largent, the second one taking the ball to the Miami 2 yard line. A shocked Miami crowd urged the Dolphins to hold, but Warner ran a sweep around right end for a touchdown. The Dolphin crowd was shocked and silent. A Miami fumble led to a Seattle field goal, making the final score Seattle 27, Miami 20. Thousands of Seahawk fans greeted the team when it landed at the Seattle airport after flying home from Miami. "Super Bowl! Super Bowl! Super Bowl!" they chanted. The Seahawks had earned the right to play the Los Angeles Raiders in Los Angeles for the AFC championship and a spot in the Super Bowl. The Seahawks had beaten the powerful Raiders both times the teams had played during the regular season. Why not make it three times?

The Raiders had other plans. They were in Kreig's face all day, forcing the Seattle quarterback to make several mistakes. Los Angeles led 30-7 before Seattle's backup quarterback, Jim Zorn, drove the Seahawks to a touchdown. It was to be Zorn's last moment in the spotlight for the Seahawks. A year later, Seattle's first pro football star would be gone.

In 1984, the Seahawks compiled a 12-2 record with two games left in the season. Kreig, who would be named to the AFC Pro Bowl squad after the year, was marvelous during that fourteen-game stretch. "Dave Kreig is just a

1 9 8 4

What an arm! Dave Krieg threw bomb after bomb for an NFL record 3,671 yards passing.

Curt Warner (#28) helped turn the Raiders upside down.

winner," Knox said. "That's all you can ask of a quarterback." Seattle needed to win only one of its last two games to claim its first AFC West title, but the Seahawks were beaten badly by both Kansas City (34-7) and Denver (31-14). Denver, not Seattle, won the AFC West. Seattle got a wildcard position in the playoffs. The Seahawks defeated the Los Angeles Raiders 13-7, and then returned to Miami for a rematch with the Dolphins. But Miami was ready this time, beating Seattle 31-10. The Seahawks had again fallen short of the Super Bowl, this time by two wins.

The following year, Seattle was picked by many experts to make it to the Super Bowl. It was a tribute to Knox's ability to coach. It was also a tribute to the team's on-field leader, Dave Kreig. As Kreig went, so went the Seahawks: when he was hot, they were hot. His teammates rallied around Kreig, and they were the first to defend him when the fans started to boo the Seattle quarterback.

When Kreig first came to the Seahawks, he was a long shot to make the NFL. In fact, he had to beg Seattle to give him a tryout. He and two other quarterbacks had free agent tryouts, but only Kreig was invited to training camp. Even so, Kreig wasn't exactly confident he'd have a career with the Seahawks. "I knew if I didn't get a break, I was going to be cut," Kreig said. An injury to quarterback Steve Myer allowed Kreig to make the team as the third and final signal caller. Two years later, he became Zorn's backup. Finally, in the middle of the 1983 season, Knox made Kreig the permanent starter. "I had been waiting for that chance for a long time," Kreig said. "And for some reason, when I got in there, the entire team began playing well."

Kreig kept the Seahawks playing well. After a disap-

1 9 8 5

Terry Taylor returned an interception seventy-five yards for a touchdown as Seattle defeated the Raiders 33-3.

23

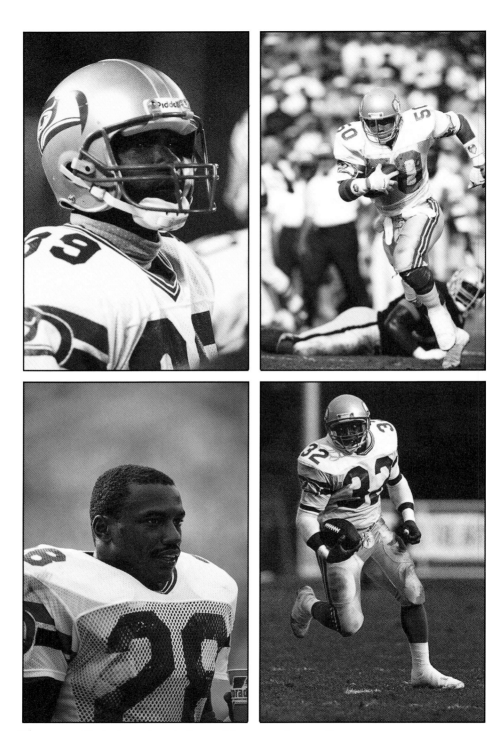

24   *Clockwise: Brian Blades, Fredd Young, John L. Williams, Curt Warner.*

pointing 8-8 season in 1985, Kreig led the team to a 10-6 record in 1986 and a 9-7 mark in 1987. The team made the playoffs in 1987, but lost in the first round to Houston.

WILLIAMS IS JOHN L. ON THE SPOT

Before the 1988 season, the Seahawks were talking about winning a championship, something the team had never done. Kreig and Largent were still stars, and Curt Warner was a good running back for the Seahawks. But there was a new star in the Seattle backfield: his name was John L. Williams. The Seahawks had drafted Williams in 1986, and he moved right into the starting lineup. Knox had wanted Williams as a blocker for Warner, and as a pass catcher. Williams proved to be much more than that.

Unlike most Seahawk stars, Williams was a first-round draft choice. Many experts thought it was strange that Seattle would use a first-round pick to take a fullback. Most teams use a fullback strictly as a blocker; others don't use one at all, adding an extra wide receiver instead. Seattle, though, uses its fullback, mostly because Williams is too good not to use. But Williams is not like most stars. He comes from a tiny town in Florida, and he is as quiet as his hometown—Palatka, Florida—is small. He is also as strong as an ox.

Chuck Knox may have paid Williams the ultimate compliment when he said, simply, "He is a football player." What Knox meant is that Williams is tough as nails. Opposing tacklers soon learned about Williams's toughness. They would try to tackle him low, and they'd get bruised by his huge legs. Or they would try to tackle him high, and they'd get hit with Williams's trademark—a stiff arm. In

1 9 8 7

"The Boz" hit the Seattle scene! Seattle's number one pick was collegiate defensive phenomenon Brian Bosworth.

Sticky fingers! John L. Williams fumbled only three times in his first 560 career possessions.

the early days of pro football, running backs would often use the stiff-arm technique—extending their arm to ward off tacklers. But Williams is one of the few modern runners to use this tactic.

Williams had a good rookie year in 1986, and he played even better in 1987. In 1988, John L. was the main man in the Seahawk offense. He gained 877 yards rushing, and he led the team in pass receptions with fifty-eight. It was the first time someone besides Steve Largent had led the Seahawks in pass catching.

The Seahawks took an 8-7 record into the regular season finale in Los Angeles against the Raiders. If the Seahawks won, they would claim their first AFC Western Division title. If they lost, they wouldn't even get into the playoffs. Williams made sure they didn't lose. The Seahawk fullback had 180 yards in pass receptions and 59 yards rushing as Seattle outscored the Raiders 43-37. To no one's surprise, it was Williams who made the key play. With the Seahawks leading 30-20 in the third quarter, Kreig rolled out to the right and threw a screen pass back across the field to Williams on the left. John L. gathered in the ball and motored seventy-five yards for a touchdown, shocking the Raiders and giving the Seahawks their first-ever division title.

Los Angeles cornerback Mike Haynes chased Williams the last 40 yards. "I'm running after the guy," Haynes said, "and he's getting farther and farther away from me. A big guy like that isn't supposed to run that fast." Williams, who's five feet eleven inches tall and weighs 220 pounds, *isn't* supposed to be that fast. And fullback isn't supposed

A strong offensive line led Williams to success.

'The Man from Milton,' Dave Kreig.

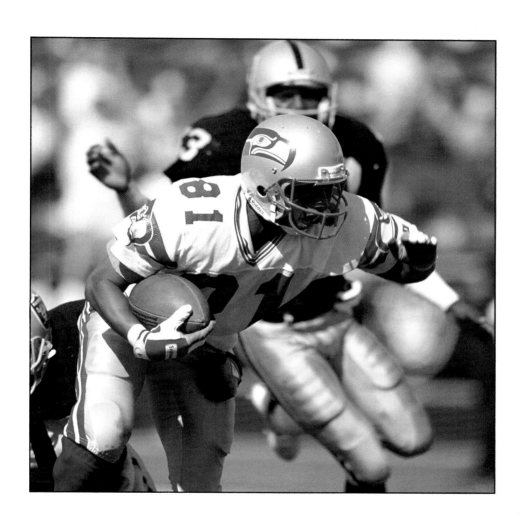

Wide receiver Tommy Kane.

Razor sharp Brian Blades cut through opposing defenses to lead the Seahawks in receiving yardage.

to be a position for a star. But John L. Williams is a star: a great combination of size, speed, strength, and pass-catching ability.

Entering the 1990s, Williams was only twenty-five years old. He is the centerpiece of the next great Seahawk team. Like all of the Seahawk stars of the past, Williams is unique. Most stars in the NFL spend the offseason traveling or making television appearances. John L. Williams goes home to rural Florida and lives with his mother in a house he bought for her. "I'm not a city type of person," Williams said. But Williams will spend the fall months in Seattle for several years to come.

The Seahawks and Williams are entering a new era. The team has a new owner, Ken Behring. He bought the Seahawks from the Nordstrom family, which had owned the team since it was formed. The team also is counting on several new, young stars to lead it to the Super Bowl. Kelly Stouffer is the quarterback of the future for the Seahawks. Stouffer will be throwing to a talented young receiver named Brian Blades, who made the Pro Bowl in only his second season in the league.

Williams, Stouffer, and Blades—remember those names. And remember a pair of linebackers, David Wyman and Rufus Porter. They will be the Seahawks' stars of today and tomorrow.